D0938928

CHASING DOPAMINE

9.3.20

Jim,
I hope you enjoy my book! Every doctor should READ this book! Please SPREAD the word on this book to the medical community.
All the BEST

DR. RICK CAMPANA, MD, FASAM

Dr. Rick Campana, MD, FASAM

ISBN 978-1-0980-4179-3 (paperback)
ISBN 978-1-0980-4180-9 (hardcover)
ISBN 978-1-0980-4181-6 (digital)

Christian Faith Publishing, Inc.
832 Park Avenue
Meadville, PA 16335
www.christianfaithpublishing.com

Printed in the United States of America

For Dr. Robert A Campana, Ph.D
(August 30, 1951 to February 12, 1996)
"Your hand guided my pen as I wrote this book"

INTRODUCTION

My name is Dr. Rick Campana, and I am a board certified addiction specialist who has been treating substance use disorders (SUDs) for the past fifteen years. This book is based on my own personal story of recovery and the stories of selected patients I have treated specifically with opioid use disorder (OUD) during the past fifteen years.

My book is brutally honest and filled with personal stories from actual patients that I have treated for addictions. This book is meant to educate people on the medical science of addiction disorders and the various treatments that are now available for a number of different types of addiction disorders. There is much misinformation among the general public and even the medical community about addiction disorders. There is also persistent stigma (black cloud) that continues to prevail with addiction disorders.

My book is directly aimed at giving factual information about the causes of addiction and the most effective evidence-based treatments that are currently available to treat a variety of addiction disorders. Medically assisted treatment (MAT) is currently the most effective treatment available to treat opioid addictions. The leading experts in addiction medicine all agree that MAT works for opioid use disorders and that it is significantly underutilized.

Doctors specializing in addiction medicine, like myself, are at the tip of the spear in dealing with the current opioid crisis in USA. As the opioid crisis continues to rise at an exponential pace, we are losing a generation of young and old people despite having very effective medical treatments that can save lives and give patients with addiction disorders a chance to have a normal productive life.

It is essential for the reader to understand that addiction disorders are a genetic brain disease influenced by psychosocial variables. The vast majority of patients I treat have opioid addictions (heroin and or pills).

The single most important thing that I personally see is essential in reducing the number of opioid overdose deaths in United States is to reduce all barriers to medically assisted treatment (MAT). Every patient who started on MAT for an opioid addiction means one less patient who will go out on the street and buy heroin laced with fentanyl (90 percent of street heroin laced with fentanyl). I will talk later in the book about fentanyl, but for now, the reader should understand that when a patient uses any illicit drug from the street, they risk having a fatal overdose due to fentanyl.

I wish this book to give people hope in knowing that addiction disorders can be overcome with effective medical and supportive lifestyle therapy.

CHAPTER 1

My Story

I was born in London, England, in December of 1955, where my parents worked for the US Embassy. We were an Italian family of four sons (I am the youngest). We moved to Williamsburg, Virginia, in 1957, in a nice neighborhood, and I had a very normal childhood. My parents were big believers in getting a good education, so they made the financial sacrifice by sending all four sons to a private Catholic school, so we could all get the best education possible. Both of my parents worked, which was not the norm back in the sixties. My dad was the scoutmaster of Troop 106 in Williamsburg, and he made sure all of his sons started in the troop at an early age.

I believe my parents were smart enough to know that it would be better for their four boys to go camping and hiking than hanging out with the other kids in the neighborhood who were getting into all kinds of trouble. Anyway, I decided at the age of ten that I wanted to become a doctor after admiring actor Robert Young who played as a family doctor on the TV show *Marcus Welby, MD*.

After declaring my future profession, I got to work in a big way academically to get the highest grades possible, even though I was not one of the smarter students in my school. Through discipline, drive, and raw determination, I was able to excel academically. I graduated early from high school and started at the College of William & Mary in 1973 and lived at home. I then decided after two semesters at William & Mary that I wanted to experience the campus resident life, so I transferred to Old Dominion University in Norfolk, Virginia. I graduated with honors from ODU and then applied to medical school. I was rejected twice, and then on my third application, I was accepted to Eastern Virginia Medical School. October 30, 1978 was one of the happiest days of my life when I got my acceptance letter to medical school. After receiving my letter of acceptance, I drove around my town endlessly for eight hours, exploding with such strong emotions, knowing that I made it into medical school, and I was now going to really become a doctor. I told myself all the hard work finally paid off.

I now know that I experienced a major surge of dopamine (the magic brain chemical that makes us happy and influences our behavior) when I opened my medical school acceptance letter. I started medical school in June of 1979 and graduated in June of 1982. Most interesting, my very last medical school rotation was working in a methadone clinic, treating heroin addiction patients.

I was always a people and family pleaser, so I decided to get married to a nurse I met during my junior year of medical school on the same day I graduated from medical school. The night before my graduation and my wedding, I took my first 10 mg Valium to help me sleep, which was the beginning of my dark journey into pharmaceutical medications.

After finishing my residency training, I opened an urgent care clinic in my hometown of Williamsburg that I ended up calling *First Med of Williamsburg*. My hometown welcome by the local community hospital was less than friendly as the hospital decided to purchase land across where I had already started to build my clinic. It became a David (me) and a Goliath (hospital) story with the obvious intentions of the local hospital to drive me out of town. I met with the hospital administrator and asked him why the hospital chose to build across the street from my clinic, and his response was, "It's a free world, and this is a business decision."

As I left the meeting with this administrator, my parting words were, "Sir, I am twenty-eight years old, and the worst that can happen to me is I go bankrupt." I also told him that I had "the fire and spirit" to make my clinic a success and I would never allow anyone, including a big hospital to drive me out of town! So two weeks after I opened my medical clinic, the local community hospital decided to sell the property they had purchased across the street, and I was now ready to set *Williamsburg on fire* by creating Williamsburg's first urgent care clinic, making it the very best urgent care clinic possible.

Once my clinic opened in April of 1984, my patient load grew quickly, and I found myself working ten to twelve hours per week, *day* sometimes seven days a week including most holidays. Initially, I had no other doctor helping me, and that was a very terrifying feeling for a young doctor just out of residency training. My dad helped me launch my clinic with his business management skills and his pocketbook (we will get to that later). Anyway, the first few years were very challenging, and for a while, it was touch and go financially. I was now the medical director, CEO, president, and all these other big titles of this clinic—and along these titles came tremendous responsibilities.

I was now in charge of taking care of my clinic, my patients, and my staff. Unfortunately, they never taught in medical school a damn thing on running a medical practice yet alone an urgent care center. I recall many nights staying at the clinic with my dad, sometimes up to midnight, just to complete all the paperwork, charting, billing, staff issues, and items of the day to keep the clinic operational.

At one point, we needed a 100K credit line to keep things running at the clinic. I went to the bank in town where I was told I have no collateral and my MD degree does not mean anything because I had no money and or assets! It was at this point when I told my dad we're not going to be able to make it financially because the bank won't give me a business credit line. The following day, my dad came to my office and handed me his deed of trust to his personal residence and told me to present this to the bank as collateral for the credit line. Of course, I said, "No way, Dad, I'm not going to put my parents' home on the line for this clinic."

He quickly responded by telling me I have to take him up on his offer as he told me, "Rick, we have a great business plan here, and

Williamsburg needs this medical clinic." With these powerful words, I took my dad's deed of trust to the bank and secured a credit line for 100K. With the 100K capital, my dad and I were able to keep First Med of Williamsburg alive; and eventually, business kicked into high gear, and I was able to repay the note off and release my parents' deed of trust from the bank.

Once my clinic was discovered by the locals and tourist visiting Williamsburg, I was working twelve to fourteen hours to see patients, complete charts, order supplies, payroll, human resources, marketing, accounting, and just about everything else that needed to be done to keep First Med alive and well. For the first five years of opening First Med, I was working seven days a week and putting in seventy-hour work weeks. The stress was, at times, overwhelming as I was the pilot in command of this clinic; and I knew that I was responsible for the care of all the patients that came in the clinic as well as my entire staff. It was a daunting responsibility running the clinic, but I was so determined to make it a successful family business, as well as a reputable medical clinic, that I sacrificed my own general wellness and health.

In the process of focusing so intensely on making my clinic a success, I soon lost touch with many of the things in life I once enjoyed, including family and friends. I became programmed to wake up in the morning, shower, dress, go to the clinic to work all day, and most of the evening, come home eat, say hello to my wife, watch TV for an hour, and go to bed. This was my routine, and there were very few breaks along the way. At times during our busy season, I would see on average fifty-five to seventy-five patients a day. Most of the patients were routine fairly straightforward problems. However, each day was sprinkled with the unexpected patient or two who presented with a multitude of complex medical problems or some type of surgical problem (chainsaw lacerations, fractured bones, dislocated shoulders, acute chest pain, acute asthma, etc.).

There were days where I was overwhelmed with trying to manage so many patients never knowing when my next surprise patient (complicated patient) would walk in the door. I kept pushing through this grind day in and day out. However, one day I came to my clinic with a terrible cough and sore throat. Hoping to find something to ease my cough and painful throat, I got a sample bottle of cough syrup from my sample closet and took one tablespoon of hydrocodone (5 mg/tsp), and within ten minutes, my throat's pain and cough were completely gone. Additionally, I experienced a very intense boost in my energy level. I then decided to finish the rest of the sample bottle of cough syrup (10 mg total more of hydrocodone). Well, for the rest of my twelve-hour shift, I was a mean, lean fighting machine multitasking, being ultra-productive, and generally having a great time once again seeing patients. It was like a "light switch" went off in my brain when I tasted hydrocodone for the first time.

As a medical student in the early eighties, I was never taught anything about addiction disorders and/or chronic pain management. The focus of my medical education was more on the "meat and potatoes" of medicine (common medical surgical problems) but very little on mental health disorders. It was standard practice in my early days as a doctor to prescribe opioids for many conditions including cough, headaches, back pain, and many other conditions that we now realize as doctors to never have been treated with opioids. Yet the pharmaceutical companies would bombard my office with samples of all kinds of drugs, including opioids. There was an endless stream of drug reps coming to my clinic to promote their wonderful medications—free lunches, all kinds of souvenirs, golf balls, etc.—to win me over to prescribe their medications.

It is common knowledge now, among my colleagues, that we got duped by Perdue Pharmaceutical who developed OxyContin (generic for oxycodone), a powerful Schedule 2 opioid. The drug reps for Perdue would visit my office and tell me how safe OxyContin was and how it had a low addiction potential since it was specially formulated to be a slow release product. At this same time, managed-care insurance companies and the internet kicked into high gear, and doctors were now being rated online through sites such as Health Grades on how well they were managing pain. The pain management doctors came up with a fifth vital sign called "level of pain management."

All doctors were then advised to asses all their patients' level of pain along with the usual pulse, BP, respirations, and temperature.

Health Grades became the measuring stick in which many doctors were awarded financially, based on their Health Grade score. I know of one ER doctor friend of mine that was fired from a medical clinic by a big corporate hospital that owned this clinic because he was not seeing enough patients per hour and his Health Grade was not high enough. To digress momentarily, I should tell you, online doctor review sites are many times grudge matches against doctors whom patients did not like personally, not because the doctor was a bad clinician. The last time I looked at my Health Grade, I had mostly four stars, but I did get a one star from a patient whom I never saw. He was upset about the wait time and left the clinic (before I could see him) very upset and wrote that I was the worst doctor he had ever seen.

Anyway, doctors soon discovered that OxyContin was indeed extremely addictive. From the OxyContin explosion, the current opioid crisis has now morphed into the heroin crisis. Years later, Perdue Pharmaceutical was convicted under False Claim Act for false claims about OxyContin to doctors, and they were fined billions.

After my first experience with hydrocodone, I was off to the races. I went from being tired all the time to having endless energy and always being in a good mood. I accomplished so much work while I was using hydrocodone, and I justified my use by saying it would only be short-term until I can hire another doctor to give me a break from the seventy-hour weekly grind. Sadly, I didn't understand the addictive potential of opioids. I had no formal training on addictions; and the general medical climate at the time was opioids were relatively safe, very effective for pain (acute and chronic), and they had low potential for abuse/addiction. With an endless supply of samples, I was able to fuel my now fully blown opioid addiction. At first, everything went well with my addiction, and I remained in denial for a long time. As with any chronic use of opioids, my tolerance level increased causing me to use higher doses of hydrocodone. I was struggling with my life at this time as my personal family life was not good. I was always working and never spending anytime with my family.

In truth, I was miserable and trapped in this viscous cycle of trying to avoid withdrawal symptoms and continue to function normally. It is said the last thing a doctor gives up when he has an addiction disorder is his work. A doctor will destroy everything else first including family, friends, passions, etc. before he destroys his professional job. I was really trapped as I could talk to no one about my addiction to opioids, including my wife, fellow colleagues, psychiatrist, or anyone else that could have helped me. I had this perfect image to live up to, and I could not let anyone know how severely addicted I had become to opioids. Ironically, I had lost one of my brothers to an opioid overdose, yet I did not know where to get help for myself with the same disease my brother was also cursed with that took his life. I did try on several occasions to check myself into a motel far away from my home and just suffer through the withdrawal symptoms.

Unfortunately, these periods of forced abstinence were to strong and left me with the worst depression anyone can imagine. So as soon as I would get back home, I would self-medicate on my opioid, and the withdrawal symptoms including the depression (mental funk) would go away and I was functional again. As my addiction disorder became worse, so did my personal life. Eventually, my wife had enough of my addiction behaviors and moved out of our house with my three children. One night after visiting my wife and kids in their new home, I over medicated myself as I was in such grief and despair; and then I stupidly tried to drive home. I was saved that night by the Virginia State Police who stopped me as I was swerving on Interstate 64 and promptly arrested me. I was taken to the local hospital's ER where I had staff privileges and drug and alcohol tested by the police. I was then taken to jail and released on bond. I realized that night that I was now in big trouble and my medical career was on the line. I also realized that I had reached my bottom, and this was the lowest point of my life. Everything I had worked so hard for was now in jeopardy. Fortunately, the Board of Medicine had a formal treatment program for doctors with addictions; and by enrolling in this program, I was able to save my medical license and get the help I needed.

Shortly after my arrest, I was sent to a drug treatment program for doctors in Tennessee. Initially, I thought I would be there for two weeks and be sent home to get back to work. I laugh now as I think of this event since I only bought two weeks of clothes with me. As I started this program, I felt a sense of relief and doom at the same time. I knew when I got back home I was going to have to deal with all the regulatory agencies that were going to come visit me. I had stepped on a major doctor land mine! Yet I was thankful I got captured and was finally able to get help. I stayed four months in residential treatment where I finally got the help and support I needed.

During my residential treatment, I became angry at myself for becoming addicted in the first place, and I made a promise to myself that I would become an expert in the diseases of addiction disorders, especially opioid addictions. I also promised God that I would use my own personal recovery along with my medical expertise in addiction medicine to help as many patients as I could who were inflicted with this same disease. After I completed my five-year recovery contract with the Virginia Board of Medicine, I took additional training in addiction medicine and eventually became a board certified/fellow in *addiction medicine* (a now recognized subspecialty by the American Board of Medical Specialties).

I actively started treating opioid addiction patients in 2004 with MAT when doctors could legally start using a drug called Suboxone (buprenorphine) that was now FDA indicated for opioid addiction disorders. Doctors were required to get special training and to be mentored by more experienced addiction doctors in order to prescribe Suboxone. Prior to starting my addiction practice, I operated an urgent care/family practice clinic starting in April of 1984. I slowly transitioned out of urgent care/family practice, and I now only practice addiction medicine. I also established, operated, and was the medical director for three methadone/Suboxone clinics for over six years.

One of my major missions in life now and a payback promise that I made to God is that I will actively advocate for evidenced-based sound medical treatments for addiction disorders by treating patients with addictions as I would any other patient with a chronic medical condition. Furthermore, I will continue my educational campaign with the legal/court system to encourage all courts across the country to treat nonviolent drug offenses as a medical condition. I am forever reminding the court system, especially probation officers that addiction is a medical disorder and treatment should take precedence over incarceration.

Throughout my book, I will interject personal stories of how my recovery started and what I have done to finally figure out how to chase the magic chemical we are all chasing called *dopamine*. I will talk in more detail about *dopamine*, but I do want to introduce everyone to this particular word as it is very important to understand how this brain chemical affects our behaviors.

CHAPTER 2

My Patients' Stories

For the last fifteen years, I have been treating patients with opioid addictions (opioid use disorders). My treatment is based on using medically assisted treatments (MAT) using three specific drugs, including buprenorphine (Suboxone), methadone, and Vivitrol (naltrexone). The first two drugs are evidenced-based treatment using long acting opioid meds to suppress withdrawal symptoms and cravings. Vivitrol is used to block the opioid receptors so that opioids won't affect the brain if patients are on Vivitrol. In this chapter, I will profile a sampling of my patients using actual patient stories from the first time I started their treatment with MAT to where they are now. All identities are protected for HIPPA purposes. These are my success stories.

I will start with my very first patient that I started treating in 2004. Patient *A* was a twenty-eight-year-old female who had become addicted to prescription opioids after being prescribed opioids by multiple doctors for fibromyalgia syndrome. She was being treated by another doctor in another state with Buprenex (buprenorphine) injections which was a form of Suboxone in an injection form used in surgical patients for pain. Buprenex was only indicated for pain at that time, but it was found to work well for patients addicted to opioids. Suboxone was not available at the time she sought treatment for

16

her opioid addiction, so she was able to find a doctor who prescribed Buprenex injections for her. Eventually, she moved to Virginia where she continued her treatment with me.

When I first started treating her, Suboxone (buprenorphine) had just been approved by the FDA and the DEA to use in treating patients with opioid addiction. Patient *A* was a single mom when I first met her, and she was a heavy cigarette smoker who also had depression and anxiety disorders. My initial impression of Patient *A* was how effectively her opioid addiction disorder was responding to buprenorphine injections. Once I switched her to Suboxone at a dose of 16 mg a day, she no longer needed the injections. I was now able to keep her stabilized on Suboxone, and she did not experience any further opioid withdrawal symptoms and or cravings. Her affect (mood) improved drastically, and she eventually completely stopped smoking cigarettes and started a regular exercise program. I initially was seeing her one a month where I would also provide psychotherapy including motivational and cognitive behavioral therapies along with relapse prevention strategies and general wellness guidelines for recovery.

I was amazed how well Patient *A* did in my program and not once did the patient ever have a positive drug screen for any non-prescribed controlled drug and or any other illicit drug. Her life continued to improve, and eventually, she married and had a few children; and she lives in a nice home with a loving husband. She continues to see me every two months, and to this day, she has never relapsed. She has embraced many of the recovery tools I have given her, and she often reminds me how I saved her life. I like to tell her as I tell all my patients, "I'm the coach, and you are the quarterback. I have some excellent plays I can give you to win this game, but only you can execute the plays I give you to achieve a meaningful recovery." I also remind my patients including Patient *A* every time I see them that "recovery is an ongoing process that each patient must respect and work on regularly." Finally, I continue to remind Patient *A* along with all of my other patients that "recovery is more than taking a pill [Suboxone], but it also is a permanent lifestyle and attitude change that takes time."

Patient *B* is my next patient who is a thirty-year-old male, severely addicted to street heroin using up to one gram of heroin intravenously daily. He worked in tree cutting (tree surgeon), and he made a good salary; but all his money was used to buy heroin. He was married with two children, and his family was heading to foreclosure on their home because he was the primary provider and all his money went to heroin. Eventually, his wife threatened divorce if he did not get treatment. When I first saw Patient *B*, he was a mess, to say the least. And he was in active opioid withdrawal after stopping methadone he had gotten from the street. He was so desperate to get help. He stopped his methadone cold turkey and went into severe withdrawals for ten days. When he came to my office thirteen years ago, he was still very sick and depressed after coming off the methadone. I started him in Suboxone 16 mg daily, and within twelve hours, he was a new man. He told me he finally had hope that he could beat his addiction once he experienced how well the Suboxone helped suppress his withdrawals and cravings. During the initial course of treatments, I learned much about this patient's psychosocial history and discovered that he too started using opioids after they were prescribed by a doctor for his back pain.

Today Patient *B* is happily married and doing well financially. He has mended all relationships with his children, and he is expecting his first grandchild soon. Each time I meet with Patient *B*, he tells me of new literature he has read on addictions. He has become extremely well informed about medically assisted treatment (MAT), and he actively advocates for its use by sharing his personal recovery story with as many people as he can. I like to refer to him as my "Point Man," leading the way on the war on opioid addictions. He thanks me each time I see him for saving his life and allowing him to reap the rewards of meaningful recovery. Since he started on Suboxone, he has never relapsed or had any positive drug screens for nonprescribed controlled medications and/or illicit street drugs.

Patient *C* is a forty-year-old male engineer with a twelve-year history of opioid addiction starting out when his PCP started him on unlimited Vicodin for his recurrent tension headaches. He was again a very straight shooter who had never used illicit drugs including cannabis. He only used alcohol on a very limited basis and he did not smoke cigarettes and he worked out regularly. He was married for many years and had three children all in college. He was the local scoutmaster of a troop in town, and he had achieved the rank of Eagle Scout in his youth; and he was awarded the Silver Beaver (the highest accomplishment a scoutmaster can achieve). When I met him, he was using up to 100 mg of Vicodin a day. He was doctor shopping and visiting the local urgent care and ERs to continue to acquire his supply of Vicodin. He finally hit bottom when he was confronted by one of the doctors in a local urgent care clinic who referred him to me for treatment of his opioid use addiction. We both clicked on our initial meeting once he told me he was a scoutmaster and that he was an Eagle Scout and he had gone to Philmont Scout Ranch. I too was very connected to the Boy Scouts as my entire family has been involved with the scouting program since the early 1960s. I started this patient on 12 mg of Suboxone, and within twenty-four hours, he was stabilized without any further opioid withdrawal symptoms and/or any cravings whatsoever. He has now been my patient for over seven years, and he has never relapsed or had a positive drug screen since he was started on Suboxone. He recently had a child at his last visit. He told me he was recently promoted and his wife and he were expecting another child.

Patient *D* is a sixty-year-old retired school teacher who started using OxyContin after her OB/GYN started prescribing her this medication for her chronic pelvic pain syndrome. She started out using Percocet 5 mg tablets at bedtime for her pain and to help her sleep. Her pelvic pain was mild at best which prompted me to question her use of Percocet pain medication. Her response was, "My doctor told me this drug would work best for my pain and only real drug addicts get addicted to it." Her doctor routinely refilled her OxyContin pain meds without any further discussions about potential addiction and/or other physical side effects.

Over the course of a few months, the patient had developed significant tolerance to her Percocet, and she was now using 60 mg of Percocet daily. She attempted several times to wean off her Percocets, but the withdrawal symptoms and depression she experienced were too much for her to handle. She finally overdosed one night after getting in a verbal altercation with her husband by taking 10 Percocet tablets and then drinking a half a bottle of Merlot. When I first met her, she was withdrawn, anxious, and very depressed. I started her on 16 mg of Suboxone, and within forty-eight hours, her affect had improved considerably; and she was no longer experiencing any withdrawal symptoms and/or cravings. I referred her to a psychiatrist to handle her General Anxiety Disorder (GAD). Over the next six months of follow up visits, this patient showed remarkable clinical improvement with her recovery. She completely stopped drinking alcohol, and she joined the local YMCA and started swimming. She has now been with me for seven years, and she continues to remain abstinent from all opioids and alcohol.

Patient *E* and *F* are a middle-aged couple who both started using prescriptions opioids to get energy during the day. This couple owned their own business, and they were financially very well off. Like many of my patients, predisposed to opioid addiction, they both rapidly increased their daily oxycodone dose from 10 mg daily to 130 to 150 mg daily. The husband had a higher tolerance, so he was consuming up to 150 mg daily and the wife at 130 mg daily. Of course, once they burned all their bridges with the local medical community, they turned to the street to purchase their oxycodone. At the time they were buying oxycodone tabs on the street, they were spending up to 300$ per day.

Patient *G* is a thirty-eight-year-old male who started treatment in my Suboxone program five years ago after he recognized he was severely addicted to heroin. At his peak addiction, he was using 1 g IV heroin (intravenously) daily. He was well-educated with multiple college degrees and has a very successful career as a defense contractor. After realizing he could not escape the hold of his heroin addiction and after he became suicidal, he researched various treatments to help him get off heroin and finally decided to start Suboxone. Once he began Suboxone treatment, his life completely changed for the better. He no longer was controlled by the endless cycle of chasing "dope sickness" and covering his tracks among family and friends. His relationships with his family improved dramatically, and he met the love of his life; and he now has a healthy three-year-old daughter along with his additional three stepdaughter and his wife. He attributes the start of his recovery to medicallyassisted treatment (MAT) and the continuation of his recovery to continue long-term maintenance using Suboxone. He has changed his attitude and lifestyle for the better, and he now embraced his recovery as the most priority of his life.

Patient *H* is a sixty-eight-year-old female who thinks she is going on thirty. She started using opioids at age fifty-four following and a slip and fall injury. She was prescribed Lora tabs (hydrocodone) for her pain and quickly developed a high tolerance causing her to use up to 60 mg hydrocodone daily. She was then switched to Fentanyl because her Lora-Tabs dose had gotten too high, and she needed a more powerful opioid to function. Actually, this patient's main problem was pain control and not actually addiction disorder. We refer to this type of patient as having "pseudo–addiction," which is when a patient demonstrates addictive behaviors (seeking pain meds) not for a high but to get pain relief. Once this patient was tapered off her prescribed opioids and started on Suboxone, she noted significant pain relief and was able to function again. She also never developed a tolerance to her Suboxone and has been at a stable dose of 8 mg a day for the past two years.

Patient *I* is a forty-five-year-old female who started in my Suboxone program ten years ago after she became addicted to Vicodin that she was prescribed by GYN and her PCP MDs for a bevy, a different problem. She is married and at the time was raising three small children with her husband. After she finally realized she could not taper off her Vicodin even after attempting multiple times, she found me by reading an article in the local newspaper about opioid use disorders and the effectiveness of MAT (Suboxone). She quickly responded to treatment with Suboxone and was stabilized on a 6 mg daily. Her life completely changed once she started in my program, and she now has been in solid recovery for over a decade. Her marriage is stronger than ever, and her kids are doing exceptionally. She has also built a successful career once she got into recovery.

Patient *J* is a thirty-year-old male who started in my Suboxone program about two years ago after several years of being addicted to oxycodone that eventually led to heroin addiction. His life was out of control, and he was having financial issues because all of his paychecks went to buying opioids (pills and heroin). He initially loved the high of being on opioids, but after twelve months of daily heroin use, he was now using heroin just to avoid the terrible heroin withdrawal symptoms and to be able to go to work and be functional. He finally came to terms with his addiction when he realized how unproductive his life had become during his active addiction. He told me he was tired of all the wasted years spent chasing his addiction instead of building his life for the future.

Once he enrolled in my Suboxone program, I started him on 16 mg Suboxone daily and his withdrawal symptoms subsided quickly even though it took six months before all the cravings completely resolved. Once enrolled in my program, he experienced a real sense of hope that he could break the shackles of his opioid addiction. Today he continues to be in my Suboxone program, and he has not relapsed since starting on Suboxone. His family life is going very nicely, and he just had his first child (a healthy baby boy). He is gainfully employed, and he is actively involved in helping other people who are struggling with heroin addiction.

Patient *K* is a forty-two-year-old male who started my Suboxone program eleven years ago after he was prescribed oxycodone following sinus surgery. He initially liked the feeling oxycodone gave him, and shortly thereafter, he had another surgery (knee) where he was prescribed Vicodin (hydrocodone) for a three-month period following his surgery. He was able to receive as many refills on his Vicodin as he requested. After he was no longer able to get his Vicodin refills from his surgeon, he was referred to a pain management specialist. He was prescribed Dilaudid on a monthly basis by his pain specialist. He was finally referred to me after his wife realized her husband was in serious trouble with his opioid addiction. He had become totally isolated from his family and his friends, and he had lost his interest in all of his favorite passions, especially hunting and fishing. Once he enrolled in my Suboxone program, he was quickly stabilized on

16 mg Suboxone daily and all of his withdrawal symptoms and cravings disappeared. He has not relapsed once since being on Suboxone, and his life has completely changed. He is doing exceptional well at his job. His personal family life couldn't be better, and he now has rekindled his passions for hunting and fishing. He recently took a trip to Alaska where he experienced the ultimate hunting and fishing experience that he continues to tell me about each time I see him at my office. He tells me he now has money to once again enjoy his passions. He is grateful for his recovery, and he is living the life that he now controls.

Patient *L* is a thirty-four-year-old male who started my Suboxone program four years ago after he became severely addicted to opioid pills and heroin at age sixteen. He continued to use heroin off and on initially for about two years, and then he started using heroin on daily basis for about one year. He went to several residential treatment programs, but upon discharge, he would always relapse on heroin. He eventually found a certified Suboxone doctor in Louisiana and was started on 16 mg Suboxone daily. Once he started Suboxone, his withdrawal symptoms and cravings completely resolved. He moved to Williamsburg three years ago and transferred into my Suboxone program. He has not relapsed once since starting Suboxone seven years ago. His life is going exceptional well. He has a great job, and he is currently engaged to the love of his life that he met in Louisiana; and they have a healthy seven-year-old daughter. He is very appreciative of being alive and healthy now, and he has promised to God that he will give payback to God for saving him by committing his life to helping others struggling with heroin addictions.

Patient *M* is a twenty-four-year-old male who started in my Suboxone program three years ago after he became addicted to heroin at age eighteen. He initially started using heroin for recreational purposes, claiming that when he snorted a line of heroin, "I became totally energized and ultra-productive." This response is quite normal in the initial phase of opioid addiction. However, as in this patient's case, he developed a tolerance quickly and soon was no longer getting energized but was just using heroin to avoid withdrawal symptoms, so he could be functional and go to work. Upon entering my program, he was started on 24 mg of Suboxone daily. And within a month, he felt completely normal. He did have a few relapses in the first month, but he realized that when he used heroin with his Suboxone, he did not feel any of the effects of heroin, so he just stopped using heroin!

He told me it was a waste of money and he was even getting high. This is one of the beneficial effects of Suboxone as it has the highest affinity for the opioid receptors in our brains. This means once the patient is on Suboxone, his opioid receptors are now blocked by the Suboxone and no other opioid can attach to the opioid receptor. Even if the patient injected heroin it will have no effect if the patient is taking Suboxone. After the first month of treatment, this patient became one of my younger *All Stars* in recovery. He now has an excellent job with the city, a significantly improved relationship with his family, a healthy relationship with his fiancée, and a new appreciation for living a healthy lifestyle. He even quit smoking cigarettes and is working out on a regular basis.

Patient *N* is a forty-one-year-old registered nurse who started in my Suboxone program five years ago after becoming addicted to prescription opioids. She first started using Vicodin after she underwent GYN surgery seven years ago. She was prescribed Vicodin #60 (5 mg tabs) after she underwent a D&C, which is a relatively simple outpatient surgery with minimal post-operative pain. Yet she was prescribed an inordinate amount of opioid pain med, as this was customary at the time for doctors. After her GYN doctor would no longer prescribe her Vicodin, she went doctor shopping. She then began visiting a number of different doctors in town for an assortment of respiratory and musculoskeletal complaints. She was prescribed large amounts of codeine cough syrup along with an assortment of different pain meds, including morphine, Dilaudid, oxycodone, tramadol. Eventually, the patient presented to my clinic complaining of a cough, specifically requesting a brand name cough syrup called Tussionex, which has hydrocodone in it. At the moment, she requested Tussionex by name, I knew she was in trouble and was addicted to prescription pain and cough meds. I brought into my private office and confronted her about my concerns of her opioid addiction. I told her I could help her by having her enroll in my Suboxone program. She agreed and I started her on 16 mg Suboxone daily. She felt significant improvement almost immediately after starting Suboxone. She was in severe withdrawal in my office at the time I inducted (started) her on Suboxone. Within thirty minutes, she felt normal and stopped feeling sick. She was stabilized on 16 mg Suboxone daily and has maintained this same dose without developing any tolerance (unlike other opioids) for the past five years. Since entering my Suboxone program, she had a healthy non-addicted baby girl. She got a couple job promotions. She stopped smoking cigarettes. She started a regular exercise program, and her relationship with others, especially her husband, have never been better.

Patient *O* is a forty-five-year-old male construction foreman who started using prescription opioid pain meds following a shoulder surgery he sustained five years ago. He quickly discovered that he loved the *high* euphoria that he experienced initially with taking Vicodin. Following his recovery from his shoulder surgery and when all of his post-operative pain had resolved and no longer had any pain pills left, he still craved the feeling he got from using Vicodin. After he had burnt out all of the doctors he could con for opioid pain med prescriptions, he started buying opioid pills on the street. He started buying Roxicodone (oxycodone) pills on the street and started at 30 mg a day. He quickly developed a tolerance over a three-month period and was using 120 mg oxycodone daily at a cost of 300$ per day. His life was in a downward spiral, and he knew he needed help. His brother, who was in recovery already from heroin addiction, referred him to my Suboxone program. I stabilized him on 12 mg Suboxone daily, and within twenty-four hours, all of his opioid withdrawal symptoms resolved; and his mood (affect) improved considerably. He has now been in my program for one year, and he tells me at each visit that "Life couldn't be better" and "I now know I am going to be okay, Dr. Campana. Thanks to you."

Patient *P* is a fifty-four-year-old male chef who started using prescription opioid pain pills following a diagnosis of back pain caused by degenerative disk disease along with moderately severe lower back arthritis. He was initially prescribed Vicodin for his back pain. He initially loved the effect the Vicodin as it gave him endless energy. While he was on the Vicodin, he told me, "My life is on a roll, and I am now able to put in fifteen hours per day at the new restaurant I just opened." After a year of opening his restaurant, his personal doctor cut off his Vicodin supply. He turned to the street as he now recalls "to feed the beast." He needed the Vicodin just to function and to continue putting in the long hours at his restaurant. He finally realized his opioid addiction was going to cost him his business, and he checked into a local residential treatment program. He left the residential treatment program after ten days against medical advice (AMA). He was referred to my Suboxone program by the residential treatment program he had checked AMA. He has been in my Suboxone program now for over sixteen years, and he has never relapsed once. He continues to do well on 8 mg Suboxone daily. He currently is happily married, gainfully employed as an executive chef, stopped smoking cigarettes, started a yoga routine, and now routinely does mindfulness therapy to help him deal with the stresses of his life. He is grateful to be in long-term recovery and credits his long-term use of Suboxone along with a solid wellness program and a completely attitude change in life.

Patient Q is a twenty-eight-year-old male construction worker who started using opioid pain pills his senior year in high school for recreational purposes. He started using opioid pain pills on a daily basis at age twenty and developed a tolerance to oxycodone, and at the peak of his use, he was consuming 120 mg oxycodone daily; and he was now snorting his oxycodone. He realized he had hit a bottom in his life when he lost a close friend to a heroin overdose. He entered my Suboxone program six years ago and was started on 16 mg Suboxone daily. His withdrawal symptoms subsided within twenty-four hours, and he was able to return to work the next day after I started him on Suboxone. Today he continues to take the same dose, and he has not relapsed once since staring in my Suboxone program. He is currently employed and running a sideline landscape business. He stopped smoking cigarettes, and he is now incorporating a strong wellness program as part of his overall recovery. He is thankful that he now has a chance to live a productive life that unfortunately, his friend who overdosed never experienced.

Patient *R* is a thirty-five-year-old male retail manager who started using prescription opioid pain pills at age twenty-three for recreational purposes. He initially would use the pain pills for party times which then shifted to using these pills for work. He experienced an intense euphoria and a high level of energy every time he took opioids. He realized he was out of control with his opioid drug use once his life became unmanageable—and he lost his job, his girlfriend, his dog, his car, and eventually, all of his dignity. He started in my program nine years ago and was stabilized on 12 mg Suboxone daily which he continues to take at this dose currently. He has not relapsed once since staring in my Suboxone program. Today he continues to be drug-free, and he had quit smoking cigarettes. He also has a solid career as a retail manager at a local food specialty store. He has two dogs, and he is in a solid loving relationship with his soon-to-be fiancée.

Patient *S* is a forty-year-old female who started using prescription opioid pain pills eighteen years ago after she took one of her husband's oxycodone pain pills. She told me she would become *Superwoman* when she would take oxycodone. She was a new mother in a new home in a new city as her husband was in the military. She was able to initially get through all of the above daily task with the help of 80 mg of oxycodone daily. She was getting her opioid pain pills from an elderly man with Sickle cell disease. She eventually realized she could not function without using her pain pills and the withdrawals symptoms from the opioid pain pills was too powerful and left the patient functionless throughout the day. After she realized her addiction to pain pills was causing her to steal, lie, and cheat just to get her daily fix, she enrolled in thirty-day residential treatment drug rehab program, but she relapsed within forty-eight hours after being discharged from the residential program.

Interestingly, she went to the local ER that night after her discharge and was given Percocet pain pills. Obviously, residential treatment did not work for this patient which is when she found my Suboxone program through an internet site called NAABT.ORG, which is a locator site to find Suboxone certified providers like myself. Today the patient has now been in my Suboxone program for the past six years. She continues to do well at 20 mg Suboxone daily. She has not relapsed once since starting in my Suboxone program. Her personal life is going exceptionally well. She recently earned a master's degree, and she is currently a resident counselor working toward her licensed professional counselor certification.

Patient T is a thirty-one-year-old male housing subcontractor who started using opioids at age twenty-two for recreational purposes. He was introduced to Roxicodone (oxycodone) pills at a party by one of his former football friends. At first, he only used Roxicodone occasionally for about one year. However, after he broke up with his girlfriend, he went into a deep depression and started using Roxicodone on a daily basis. He quickly developed a tolerance and was snorting 150 mg of Roxicodone pills a day. He was spending $1000 a week to purchase his Roxicodone pills. He was finally intervened by his close friends and family when everyone around him realized he was addicted to Roxicodone pills. His parents stopped supporting him after they realized he was spending a small fortune on Roxicodone pills. He was referred to my Suboxone practice by a friend who was already one of my regular Suboxone patients. He was started on 20 mg Suboxone and he quickly stabilized, and all of his withdrawal symptoms subsided. He has now been in my program for the past three years, and he has never relapsed once since starting my program. He currently is in a healthy relationship with his girlfriend, and he has won back the trust of his family, especially his mom and dad. He is gainfully employed, and he now tells me, "I always have money now." He tells me "Life is good." And he looks forward to each day and all the new adventures awaiting him in his life.

Patient U is a forty-three-year-old female schoolteacher who started using prescription opioids after she underwent gallbladder surgery fifteen years ago. She had developed postpartum depression along with a gallbladder problem. She quickly discovered that Percocet eased her depression symptoms and gave her endless energy. Due to her continued post-op gallbladder complications, she was prescribed large amounts of Percocet's for pancreatic and bile duct

28

issues. Her doctors eventually cut off her supply of Percocet, and she resorted to local doctor shopping. She eventually developed such a high tolerance to Percocet that she was up to 170 mg of Percocet's daily. Her husband and her father eventually intervened after she relapsed following a twenty-one-day stay at a local residential drug treatment program. She was referred to my Suboxone program after her father read an article about the success patients were finding with Suboxone treatment. She has now been in my program for the past twelve years, and her current dose is 24 mg Suboxone daily. She has never relapsed since starting my program. Her relationships with her husband, her family, and her students have never been better. She is grateful to be alive and free of the shackles of her Percocet addiction.

Patient *V* is a twenty-nine-year-old male maintenance worker for a local museum who started using opioids after he was prescribed oxycodone for a fractured shoulder requiring surgery about seven years ago. He was given multiple refills on his oxycodone each time he was his orthopedic surgeon. Eventually, his orthopedic surgeon cut off his supply of oxycodone. After he could no longer get oxycodone through a doctor, he started buying oxycodone from a friend whose grandmother was prescribed oxycodone for a chronic pain syndrome. He continued to increase the amount of oxycodone he was taking as he quickly developed a tolerance. His maximum daily oxycodone use was 150 mg per day. Due to the cost of buying oxycodone from his friend, the patient decided to start buying heroin on the street which was much cheaper. He initially only snorted heroin, but after a few weeks, his nose was so inflamed that he could no longer get high with snorting. He then found the needle and was instructed on how to inject himself with heroin. The patient was using up to 1 g of heroin daily, and his life was now completely out of control. He was referred to my Suboxone program by a friend who was already in my program. I started the patient on 16 mg Suboxone daily, and within twelve hours, he felt normal. His withdrawals symptoms completely subsided. He no longer had cravings for opioids, and his mood and affect greatly improved. He has now been in my Suboxone program for over two years, and he has never relapsed since starting Suboxone. He now has a good job, and he never misses a day of work now. He is in a healthy relationship with his fiancée. He now has money that he can use to enjoy his hobbies. He tells me that now he is so happy to not have any opioid withdrawal symptoms and cravings. He is living each day to the fullest, and he has a new appreciation for the meaning of recovery.

Patient W is a thirty-two-year-old male HVAC service technician who started using opioids in 2006 after he was involved in a motor vehicle accident (MVA). After his first dose of hydrocodone, he noticed he would get energized quickly and he would experience a very strong euphoric feeling. Eventually, he was no longer able to get any additional refills on his Vicodin, so he turned to the street and family members. He eventually was consuming 50 mg of hydrocodone daily. He never snorted or injected his opioids and only took them by mouth. He was now spending $150 per day, which consumed most of his regular paycheck. After his wife realized their financial crisis due to him spending all of his money on opioid pills, she arranged an intervention with the rest of the patient's family. Once the patient had been intervened by his family, he was referred to my Suboxone program. I started him on 16 mg Suboxone daily, and he almost immediately started feeling normal; and his withdrawal symptoms resolved completely. He has been in my Suboxone program, along with his dad and sister, for the past ten years. His story underlies the strong genetic association with opioid addiction disorder. He currently is taking 6 mg Suboxone daily and is doing exceptionally well. He has never relapsed since entering my Suboxone program, and he stopped smoking cigarettes. He is happily married with one healthy ten-year-old son. He is doing well financially and is once again enjoying his passions for hunting and saving rescue shelter dogs.

Patient X is a thirty-six-year-old male successful business owner who started using opioids as a junior in high school for recreational purposes. He told me that when he took a Percocet 5 mg tablet for the first time, he lit up like a firecracker (similar to my first opioid experience). In the beginning of his opioid use, he would only take Percocet on an occasional basis. It wasn't until a decade later that he started using opioids on a daily regular basis. He quickly progressed to 150 mg of oxycodone a day at a cost of 1$/mg price tag. He maintained this lifestyle for two more years until he finally hit rock bottom both financially and emotionally. He enrolled in a Suboxone program in Denver and was started on 16 mg Suboxone daily. He was able to function and work once starting Suboxone. He then transferred to my Suboxone program once he moved to Williamsburg, and he has been in my program for the past six years. He has never relapsed once since staring Suboxone. His business is doing exceptionally well, and he just moved into a new home. He is grateful to be alive and to be freed from the lifestyle of chasing opioid drugs to avoid *dope* sickness. He also has a newfound appreciation for taking one day at a time.

Patient *Y* is a thirty-five-year-old male entrepreneur who started using opioids for fifteen years for recreational purposes. He loved the high that opioids would give him and described the feeling as "floating on a euphoric cloud." He initially used the opioid pain pills once every couple of months. He was then introduced to stronger opioids (Roxicodone 30 mg tabs), and this progresses to street heroin once he could no longer find Roxicodone pills. He eventually got up to using 2 g of heroin per day at $600 per day. He used all of his savings and then realized at this point he was going to lose everything if he did not get help. He was referred to my Suboxone program by a friend who was also in my program. I started him on 12 mg Suboxone and which worked very well for him and resolved his withdrawal symptoms and his cravings. He currently is on 8 mg Suboxone daily and is doing exceptional well with no relapses since starting my program. Today his business is going well, and he now has peace of mind knowing that he can get up every day without having to worry about getting drugs or going through withdrawal and the mental depression that he experienced when he would try to stop using heroin. He has confidence that he can maintain his abstinence from heroin and live a productive life. Thanks to his Suboxone maintenance dose.

Patient *Z* is a forty-one-year-old female pharmaceutical executive who started using opioids five years ago after she was diagnosed with migraines. She had failed other medications to deal with her migraines, and she found opioids worked best to migraine pain. She began to take opioids daily about four years ago and quickly developed a tolerance to where she was taking 60 mg of Vicodin daily. She was now using the Vicodin to deal with her migraines as well her opioid withdrawal symptoms. She needed to take Vicodin every day just to be functional and get through her day. She made multiple attempts on her own to stop her Vicodin, but she could not deal with the severe withdrawal symptoms or the terrible depression. She was referred to my Suboxone program by her therapist. I started her on 8 mg Suboxone daily. Once she was stabilized on Suboxone, she became fully functional, was able to care for her children, and she had a new appreciation for life. She has now been in my Suboxone program for two years, and she has never relapsed once since starting my program. She is happily married with three healthy children, and she is grateful to be alive and back in control of her life.

As you can see from my patients *A* through *Z*, they are all current success stories who are alive and well today because of long-term Suboxone maintenance therapy. I am convinced that a significant number of my patients *A* through *Z* would not be alive today if it were not for MAT (Suboxone/methadone). Yet sadly, I have had many casualties along the way, including far too many heroin overdoses. I have had patients that started out great in my Suboxone and methadone programs. However, due to a variety of barriers to treatment (I have dedicated a chapter to this topic), I lost them back to the street where they again starting using heroin. A number of these patients either overdosed and died, or ended up being incarcerated, or developed serious medical complications due to their continued use of heroin. The cost to for treating medical complications of active addiction disorders is enormous, not to mention the societal cost. For every dollar spent in active treatment disorders, the savings in health-related cost is $7. It's not hard to understand that MAT used to treat opioid disorders not only saves lives, but it also saves a ton of money.

CHAPTER 3

The Basics of Addiction

Addiction touches the lives of most Americans, either directly or through our friends and/or family members. All addictions share a common definition of a behavioral syndrome characterized by the repeated, compulsive seeking, or use of a substance despite adverse social, psychological and/or physical consequences, along with the physical need for an increased amount of a substance as time goes on to achieve the same desired effect. Addiction is often (but not always, as with an addiction to gambling) accompanied by physical tolerance, dependence, and withdrawal syndrome.

Opioid dependence is much more common than you may think. Men and women of all ages, races, ethnic groups, and education levels become dependent on opioids. Misuse of narcotic pain medications has increased dramatically from 1970 to the present date. More young people than ever underage eighteen are experimenting with opioids. In Williamsburg alone, I have seen many young people abusing prescription narcotics such as Vicodin, Percocet, and OxyContin for recreational use. Many of these young people have gotten their drugs off the street, online, and/or from the medicine cabinets of family and friends. I have also been seeing many young people using heroin which is readily available off the street and is now relatively inexpensive and of high purity. Sadly, many of the youth who start using heroin early in their lives quickly move to injecting it to maximize their high creating an additional set of problems, including hepatitis C, serious skin infections, blood clots, and/ or death. Surprisingly, many of my local heroin addicted patients come from gated communities and/or affluent families.

Initially, opioids cause an intense euphoria (a high) in susceptible individuals leading to a high reinforcement potential increasing the likelihood of repeated use. If you are one of those individuals who has a genetic predisposition and the right social environment to addiction, even minimal experimentation with opioids can quickly lead to full blown addiction. Clearly, people who have other blood relatives with specific addiction disorders are at a much higher risk of addiction. The initial reaction you get from taking opioids is another important determinant in those patients who become addicted. People who report feeling "energized" and "the best I ever felt" when taking opioids are at much greater risk for addiction compared to those people who do not experience these feelings when taking opioids.

It is important to understand the difference between physical dependency and addiction. Physical dependency is a normal expected reaction to prolonged use of narcotics. Any patient who takes opioids for extended periods of time will develop tolerance (need for more drug to achieve the same effect). Also, all patients taking opioids for prolonged periods will experience a withdrawal syndrome (adverse physiological effect) if the blood/tissue concentration of the opioid declines too quickly. Physical dependence is normal physiology and does not require any treatment other than slow tapering off the drug once the pain condition has subsided.

Addiction is the next step beyond physical dependence and occurs when opioid use continues after the pain subsides and/ or despite negative consequences, such as loss of a job, legal consequences, etc. Addiction causes intense cravings and a compulsive need to use narcotics without a therapeutic indication. Unlike physical dependence, addiction requires long-term treatment aimed at changing compulsive behavior and convincing patients that they do not need narcotics for survival. The physical withdrawal of opioid addiction is relatively easy to treat, but the strong cravings and compulsion for continued opiate use are the most challenging aspects of treatment.

Addiction is never intentional but rather an insidious process of rationalization and self-denial that slowly causes a patient to lose control and to become totally preoccupied with acquiring and using their opiate of abuse. As the disease progresses, patients will do whatever it takes to acquire their drug, even if it involves criminal and/or socially unacceptable behaviors. The general public labels these behaviors as weakness, immoral, destructive, manipulative, and selfish where the addicted patient sees it as survival.

Many opioid addicted patients feel trapped because they feel intense shame fostered by the stigma and public ignorance of this disease. Therefore, if we wish to effectively deal with opioid addiction (or for that matter any addictive disorder), we *must* eliminate the stigma by educating the public on the disease model of addiction and emphasize the significant breakthrough treatments that are currently available in treating opioid addiction.

CHAPTER 4

Medically Assisted Treatment (MAT)

Opioid Addiction Treatment

Our brains have opioid receptors (receptacles) that become activated when opioid drugs (plugs) dock into the receptor sites. Once the connection is made between the receptor and an opioid drug, an electrical impulse is sent down a series of nerve pathways to specific areas in our brain, causing the opioid effect (euphoria, analgesia, stress relief). Current research in drug treatment is aimed at manipulating the receptor sites with drugs that "trick our brain receptors to stabilize;" thus, reducing the withdrawal symptoms and cravings that make it so difficult for people to stop using mood altering drugs. Once the brain is stabilized, a patient can then start behavioral therapy to alter the behaviors acquired while they were actively dependent on their opioid of abuse.

Currently, there are two FDA-approved drugs for replacement therapy including methadone and buprenorphine. Methadone has been in use for a number of years while buprenorphine is a relatively new drug (approved for use in 2002). Both drugs work by stabilizing the opioid receptor in the brain. Methadone is a pure opioid receptor agonist, meaning, it is a perfect fit (plug) into the receptor (receptacle) causing complete (one-to-one) stimulation of the receptor.

Buprenorphine is a partial agonist-antagonist, meaning it causes an imperfect fit causing incomplete (limited) stimulation of the receptor. Though both drugs effectively eliminate withdrawal symptoms and cravings, buprenorphine is much safer because you can only stimulate the receptor to a certain point before achieving a plateau effect (no further effect with increasing the dose). The one-to-one stimulating effect of methadone causes a much greater risk of potential complications, including respiratory and circulatory collapse. Other clinically significant advantages of buprenorphine in addition to its safety profile, include: 1) No tolerance effect; thus, reducing the need for increasing doses to achieve the desired result. 2) No euphoric effect or cognition changes (no altered consciousness and/or diminished mental acuity). 3) The antagonist (blocking) effect of buprenorphine makes it virtually impossible for other opioids to attach to the opioid receptor sites; thus, blocking any reinforcing effect of the opioid of abuse. 4) Buprenorphine can be prescribed by a qualified MD in his/her office without the need for patients to travel to a federally designated methadone clinic, and buprenorphine can be prescribed for periods of thirty to sixty days, unlike methadone which generally requires daily visits to the clinic for administration of a single daily dose. 5) Diversion of buprenorphine to the *street* is much lower compared to methadone.

Any successful opioid treatment plan must be tailored to the individual needs of each patient. Many patients have comorbid conditions (depression, bipolar disorder, general anxiety disorders, etc.) that must be treated separately from their primary addiction. Failure to properly identify and treat a patient's comorbid condition(s) will significantly reduce their chance of prolonged recovery from their opioid dependency. Patients must feel comfortable in their treatment setting and not be made to feel like they are lepers or rejects of society. When I initially meet my opioid-dependent patients, I tell them to leave their shame and guilt at my front door. I advise them that they have a genetically inherited brain disease influenced by their social environment and that I view them on the same level as my medical patients (diabetics, hypertensive, heart disease, etc.). Once a patient understands the biosocial aspects of their addiction, the vast majority of them vigorously embrace treatment and end up doing quite well. I have found that opioid-dependent patients require a minimum of six months of buprenorphine treatment in order for them to achieve meaningful results with their behavioral therapy. Anything short of this time period usually results in relapse.

Finally, I strongly believe that general wellness must be integrated into any standard opiate treatment program including regular exercise, diet, and stress management. I have discovered that many opioid-dependent patients smoke cigarettes and live unhealthy lifestyles. Those patients who embrace a healthy lifestyle typically do much better with their recovery. As a side note, I have had much success using the new smoking cessation drug called Chantix for helping my patients stop smoking. Chantix has properties similar to buprenorphine and is very effective in stabilizing the nicotine brain receptors, preventing withdrawal symptoms and cravings while completely blocking the nicotine receptors; thus, eliminating positive reinforcing effects from smoking.

In summary, optimal treatment for opiate addiction should include an individualized tailored program that incorporates: 1) Buprenorphine to stabilize the brain (controlling withdrawal symptoms, cravings, and to block any reinforcing effects of the abused opioid drug) 2) evaluation and treatment for any comorbid conditions by a qualified mental health professional. 3) behavioral therapy to address triggers, stress management, and coping skills 4) a wellness program emphasizing healthy lifestyle choices.

CHAPTER 5

Wellness as a Part of Recovery

A major part of my own personal recovery treatment has been exercise. It is a well-known medical fact that exercise elevates brain dopamine along with many other physiological benefits to the body. I was a runner in medical school, and I found running really helped with the stress of being a medical student. However, once I started my practice, I had no time to exercise. And so I started chasing dopamine through a variety of chemicals and behaviors, including nicotine, caffeine, alcohol, opioids, gambling, and high-risk, adrenaline-producing activities. Through time, I suffered the negative effects of chasing brain dopamine on the left side of the equation (the wrong side). My left-sided addictions almost killed me until I finally realized I had to find a different way to chase brain dopamine. So I forced myself to start exercising again by running on my elliptical machine. At first, I hated it, but I knew if I could discipline myself for six months to run daily, I would start to experience elevated brain dopamine levels along with cardiovascular conditioning. After six months, I really started feeling the exercise effect on my general sense of well-being. My baseline affect (mood) had moved up two clicks, and I noticed I was much happier and my memory worked better than ever. I also became better at stress level management and engaging in conversation with others. I eventually started eating much healthier (thanks to my beautiful Ukrainian wife Galina Campana). I stopped drinking any type of soda (both diet and regular) and found I enjoyed drinking Pellegrino water. I lost over 52 lbs since I started running, and I now run 60 plus mi weekly on my elliptical. I also lift weights and do daily yoga.

For many years, even after I was no longer using drugs, I would find myself wanting to eat all the time. I would have flashbacks when I was a skinny little kid visiting my grandma in Brooklyn, New York, who would tell me, "Ricky, you're too skinny. Please eat the cream puffs I bought you." I then justified my eating six ice cream sandwiches a night as okay because they were better and safer than drugs. It took me awhile to understand how to condition my brain to control my impulsive behaviors.

I regularly tell my patients that there are two important areas of the brain that control addiction behaviors. The prefrontal cortex, which is located in the front part of your skull and the mesolimbic reward area located in the deep mid part of your brain. There are electrical connections between these two areas of the brain similar to telephone wires. The prefrontal cortex is the common sense control center of the brain that normally sends signals to the mesolimbic reward area to be sensible and not do anything stupid like eating six ice cream sandwiches nightly or putting a needle in your arm filled with street heroin filled with fentanyl. In active addiction states, the electrical connections between the prefrontal cortex of the brain and the mesolimbic reward area stop communicating with each other. The impulsive mesolimbic reward area loses all parental control from the prefrontal cortex and goes off on unrestricted impulsive behaviors. In treating opioid addictions, it is important to stabilize the mesolimbic reward area of brain by MAT so that the receptors in the mesolimbic reward area are calm and not causing a patient to experience withdrawal symptoms or cravings. Once the brain is stabilized and the patient is no longer using opioids, cognitive behavioral therapy helps to restore the electrical connections between the prefrontal cortex and the mesolimbic reward area. In time, the prefrontal cortex regains control of the mesolimbic reward area and the patient gains control over impulsive behaviors.

Another concept of recovery I teach my patients is learning how to change unhealthy conditioned behaviors. The brain will continue conscious repetitive behaviors, like putting a cigarette in your mouth two hundred times a day for a single pack a day smoker. Eventually, the behavior becomes so chronic that your brain starts to act subconsciously leading to triggered behaviors, like impulsively putting a cigarette in your mouth without even thinking of it. I teach patients how to convert bad-conditioned behaviors into good-conditioned behaviors. For my cigarette smokers, I start with having them substitute hand-to-mouth cigarette behavior to hand-to-mouth carrot/candy/or other healthy item to mouth. It is truly amazing how a patient can change behaviors if they make a conscious effort to identify the bad behavior and the good behavior, and then they can consciously train their brain with practice to eventually eliminate the bad unhealthy behavior

In my own personal recovery, I would identify and list my unhealthy behaviors, and then I would tell myself these are the healthy behaviors I want to start substituting for my bad unhealthy behaviors. For example, I would eat four to six Nutty Buddies a night which I clearly identified a bad unhealthy behavior. Next, I would identify the good healthy behavior I wanted to substitute for the bad unhealthy behavior. In the case of my Nutty Buddy addiction, I would start the transition by substituting one Nutty Buddy for a carrot stick. Over a three-week period, I was able to completely taper off the Nutty Buddies and eat carrots in place of the Nutty Buddies. All types of unhealthy behaviors can be modified over time, but it requires patience and time. Once a patient starts to feel the beneficial effects of the good healthy behaviors, their brain dopamine levels starts to rise which further reinforces the good feeling the patient experiences.

At each patient visit, I stress the importance of chasing dopamine on the right side of the equation (the good way) and avoiding the left side of equation (the wrong way). I explain how important brain dopamine levels are to experiencing a sense of well-being. I tell my patients there are six main brain dopamine elevators of the right side of the equation, including 1) sex and intimacy, 2) food, 3) humor/laughter, 4) music, 5) exercise; and 6) passions.

Each one of these categories will considerably elevate brain dopamine levels. The most powerful elevator of dopamine is passions. I will ask my patients what makes them the happiest, and they all seem to focus on their passions. The majority of my patients, prior to starting in my Suboxone program, had given up their passions. I explain to my patients once they become addicted to opioids/other substances, they no longer have time to pursue their passions because the reward areas of their brain have become *hijacked* by their drug. Now the drug controls all of the patient's behaviors as basic survival become the number one priority of the patient. The patient's day becomes consumed with chasing their drug, finding money to pay for it (through legal and illegal activities), getting a ride to their dealers, etc. It is exhausting to stay in active addiction, and it is a full-time job! Once I am able to start a patient on Suboxone, things start to change quickly. First and foremost, the opioid withdrawal symptoms subside very quickly; and once the patient is feeling physically better, they are much more able to start working a solid recovery program. I am still amazed to this day how effective Suboxone is in resolving withdrawals symptoms and cravings. Most of my patients on a stable maintenance level of Suboxone have no cravings for opioids.

Once I have the patient stabilized on Suboxone, I start addressing the patients' other addictions, especially to cigarettes, which I refer to as the *worst addiction known to mankind*!! I constantly refer to the left and right sides of dopamine equation. I tell the patient to take baby steps at first by trying to experiment with weaning of their left side equation behaviors while trying to shit to the right-side equation behaviors. I tell them they have to be patient but persistent. I tell them the right side of the dopamine equation takes longer to kick in than the left side of the dopamine equation. However, by choosing to chase dopamine on the right-side dopamine equation, they will get all of the benefits of elevation brain dopamine, along with all of the positive physical and mental health benefits as well. I share with my patients my own story of learning how to chase dopamine on the right-side equation. I tell them how I was an insulin-dependent diabetic who was obese and out of shape. One day I decided I no longer wanted to be on insulin, so I started running. I joke with my patients that I turned into a Forrest Gump, and I just keep running and I haven't stopped yet. I also like to tell my patients that exercise is the closest thing to the Fountain of Youth and if they will start some type of exercise program, they will physically look better as well as feel better.

I feel it is important in this book to include an understanding the role alternative treatments play in treating addiction disorders in lieu of pharma medications. Most specifically, how CBD/Cannabis can help patients with a variety of addiction disorders ranging from nicotine addiction, general anxiety disorders (GAD), post-traumatic stress disorders (PTSD), chronic pain syndromes, insomnia, and eating disorders. I am currently certified by the Virginia Board of Pharmacy to issue CBD/THC certificates to patients. This certificate allows a patient to go to one of five dispensaries that will soon be opening in Virginia. A patient will be allowed to get CBD oil and/or 5 percent THC oil. The patient will pay a $50 registration fee, and on the initial visit, the patient must go to the dispensary.

After the first visit (as I understand it), the patient can receive further supplies of CBD/THC oil by mail. When I issue a CBD/TCH certificate to my patients, I explain to them that I am discussing the therapeutic side of cannabis only and not the recreational side. I start my conversation by discussing the endocannabinoid system and how this system works in our bodies. I explain that the endocannabinoid system is the body's ultimate thermostat that regulates all the other major body systems. It regulates all the other smaller thermostats that control a variety of body functions including hunger, sleep, body temperature, mood, pain, and anxiety. The endocannabinoid system is located throughout the body, including the brain.

Throughout, the endocannabinoid system are millions of receptors (like electrical receptacles) that include two specific receptor sites designated for CBD and THC molecules. When the CBD or THC plug into their specific receptor sites, they trigger a chemical and neurological reaction, sending messages to certain areas of brain and other parts of the body. CBD does not affect the brain in most patients as it contains less than .3 percent THC, which is too small a concentration to cause any psychotropic effect (a high). CBD is especially good in treating pain syndromes, both acute and chronic types of pain. It has minimal to no side effects, and there is no ceiling to dosing, which means it can be dosed as high as needed. There is no tolerance, and once the patient has determined their daily CBD dose, they do not to raise the dose higher. I generally start patients on 20 mg of CBD oil sublingually at bedtime (under their tongue) and have them hold under their tongue for two to five minutes. I have them raise the dose every third night by 20 mg if they had not achieved a therapeutic effect at lower dose. Most patients will respond to doses between 20 to 60 mg per night. Not every patient will respond to CBD, but in my patient population, many do achieve a significant therapeutic response once the right dose is established.

When recommending THC oil, I explain to my patients it has a small amount of THC which is the psychotropic part of cannabinoids (it can cause patients to get high). I further explain to them that I *do not* recommend THC oil for any patient younger than twenty-five years of age because the brain is not fully developed until age twenty-five, and THC can affect developing memory areas of the brain. I also explain that each patient must discover which of these oils works best for them at their optimal daily dose. I have many patients with both opioid use disorder and chronic pain syndromes. Many of my patients became addicted to opioids after they were prescribed opioids for pain. I am convinced that CBD/THC can be used as an alternative pain reliever in many instances where patients are pre-scribed opioids. CBD/THC can effectively be used to treat a variety of acute and chronic inflammatory conditions and offer a much safer treatment then the commonly used over the counter (OTC) drugs such as Motrin/Advil (ibuprofen) and Aleve (Naprosyn). This group of drugs is referred to as nonsteroidal anti-inflammatory drugs (NSAIDs).

Chronic use of the NSAIDs can cause a variety of serious problems including gastric ulcers, kidney failure, heart attacks, and strokes. Yet NSAIDs are recommended like candy by doctors despite their significant side effects. There is much deception in pharmaceutical advertising, and people are too quick to take a pill instead of making a significant lifestyle change. I have a number of my patients who were successfully able to get of all medications (both prescribed and OTC) with a combination of Cannabis (THC or CBD) and lifestyle changes including diet and exercise.

Like recovery, wellness requires a commitment by the patient. Once MAT is combined with wellness, the results are sometimes overwhelming. Of those patients who changed their lifestyles by eating healthier, eating lighter, and exercising regularly, the clinical benefits to this group of patients is very impressive. I like to stress to all of my patients, you are never too old to start an exercise program. Exercise is key to maintaining a healthy lifestyle as well as brain dopamine levels. I tell patients, "Start low and go slow, but make exercise from this point forward in your life your new addiction!"

CHAPTER 6

Barriers to Treatment

I never realized the stigma and ignorance in the medical profession in regard to treating addiction disorders. My medical training along with most of my medical school classmates never had one class in treating addiction disorders. Our pain management instruction was also willfully deficient in helping us manage patients with chronic pain syndromes. As in any profession, there are always a few bad apples that make the majority of good doctors look bad. Addiction medicine has been the stepchild among the medical specialties and until recently was not formally recognized as a bona fide specialty. However, addiction medicine is now a recognized specialty as of 2016 when it became a member of the American Board of Medical Specialties.

Despite the push to increase the number of doctors in addiction medicine, there is still a major shortage in addiction medicine doctors due to the general stigma of treating addiction disorders and the low reimbursements compared to the other medical specialties. The reason so few doctors chose to practice addiction medicine is due to the over regulation of MAT by state and regulatory agencies. In order to prescribe Suboxone (buprenorphine), a licensed physician must complete eight hours of specialized training in using Suboxone. Once a doctor has completed this training, he is required to register with the Drug Enforcement Agency (DEA) and obtain a special X number that specifically allows Suboxone certified doctors to pre-scribed Suboxone. No other doctor, even those doctors with regular DEA licenses, are able to prescribe Suboxone for opioid use disorders.

When a doctor first receives his X number to prescribed Suboxone, the DEA limits the initial number of patients (thirty patients) a Suboxone certified doctor can treat at one time. After a year, a Suboxone-certified doctor can treat up to a hundred patients and no more. Doctors like me who are board certified in addiction medicine can treat up to 275 patients at any one time. When a doctor gets his X number from the DEA, he/she gets a letter from the DEA advising the provider that if they use their X number to prescribed Suboxone, they will be guaranteed random audits by the DEA. The DEA letter further states that the Suboxone certified provider can chose not to prescribe Suboxone and no DEA audits will occur. I can personally tell you the DEA is not the average doctor's friend, and most of my colleagues who had received X number certification to prescribe Suboxone chose not to because they did not want the hassle of dealing with the DEA. I have had two unannounced visits from DEA agents to audit my Suboxone practice. The initial visit by the DEA was fairly straightforward with two agents that were respect-ful of my time and were very professional. They spent several hours in my office reviewing my Suboxone patient records and generally reviewing my treatment protocols. They left without incident and advised me I was in full compliance with my Suboxone treatment program.

Years later, I was visited by two more DEA agents to again review my Suboxone practice. Once again, these two DEA agents made an unannounced visit to my practice and asked to review my Suboxone patient charts. All was good until one of the agents asked me about my drug samples that the pharmaceutical reps bring to my office. I discovered they were concerned about twenty cough tablets containing hydrocodone. I explained to the two DEA agents that the samples, including some cough medications with opioid, are given to tourist who visit my office as a courtesy. My office only accepted a limited amount of drug samples, especially samples that were scheduled. Anyway, one of the DEA agents confronted me and asked if I had done an inventory count of my samples. When I replied that I was unaware of this requirement, one of the DEA agents accused me of taking the cough medication samples for myself. I immediately advised both of the DEA agents to leave my office at once and to contact my attorney if they had any further questions. I was so pissed at these two DEA agents for acting so indignant and disrespectful to me. When I shared this story with other doctor friends of mine, their responses included, "Rick, you are crazy prescribing Suboxone not worth the DEA aggravation" or "Why do you want to invite the DEA into your office?" The DEA continues to unnecessarily intimidate doctors; and in my opinion, the DEA is one of the major barriers in MAT.

Other barriers to treatment include excessive amount of documentation and paperwork required to treat patients with OUD. I was the medical director and owner of a methadone clinic for six years and the amount of regulatory overload was exhausting. I used to ask my partner why we are the only two doctors in the state of Virginia who own a methadone clinic, and I soon found out once my methadone clinic opened its doors. From the very start of the clinic, we were inundated with countless rules and regulations. We were frequently threatened by a number of regulatory agencies that we could be shut down if we violated any of the rules. Okay, I am a reasonable man, but in just the regulation requirements alone, operating is a very difficult to be privately owned and operated by individual doctors. Of course, big corporate entities have the resources and financial clout to play the regulatory game. As in all areas of medicine, consolidation of methadone clinics has led to a few big players in the game with profit as their bottom line.

Endless pre-authorizations required by insurance companies for Suboxone and other addiction medications create major inconvenience for both the provider and the patient. I have had a number of patients have to wait for a week or longer to get approval for their medications. I have tried to explain to several insurance companies that Suboxone can't be interrupted as patients will go into withdrawal and relapse. I likened Suboxone to insulin. Patients receiving these medications can't have any interruptions in their daily medication regimens. Yet insurance companies put a much higher priority in approving insulin than they do in approving Suboxone. Clearly, there is a stigma with addiction medicines that still goes on today despite their life-saving qualities and evidence-based effectiveness in treating OUD.

Cost is another major barrier in treatment as many of the patients with OUD are unemployed and without insurance. An average 16 mg Suboxone daily dose cost between $7 to $15 depending on what formulation the patient is prescribed. Despite Suboxone going generic, the cost of this medication is still unreasonably high. Big pharmacies are interested in profit and not necessarily what is in the best interest of the patient.

Availability is another barrier to treatment as there the limited providers in addiction medicine, so patients are forced to travel long distances to get help. Rural areas are especially prone to this problem as some counties in United States have no providers prescribing Suboxone or any other addiction medicine services. I personally have patients who drive over two hours each way to come see me.

One of my patients told me that she has endless problems with getting her medication covered each month. Recently, her insurance company (which had covered the cost of her Suboxone) denied her claim suddenly and without written notification. This patient then had to use her own money, even though she was on limited budget to cover her meds. Patient had contacted the customer service representative for her insurance company to discuss the denial. She was told by insurance representative that "I [Dr. Rick Campana] was not licensed to prescribe Suboxone in the State of Virginia." Obviously, she was given misinformation as I am certified to treat up to 275 Suboxone patients at any one time. What the representative should have said to my patient was, "Dr. Campana does participate with your insurance plan. And therefore, we cannot honor his rx for your Suboxone."

There are many other barriers to treatment that go beyond this book, but I have highlighted some of the major barriers. Here are some solid solutions to this barrier to treatment problem we face in addiction medicine. First and foremost, define all addiction disorders as progressive chronic brain disease that can be very effectively treated with MAT along with counseling, lifestyle changes (including attitude and wellness), and effective treatments of any comorbid mental health issues (these must be treated from addiction use disorders) that concur with patients' addiction use disorders. Once we accept addiction disorders as legitimate, we can start structuring treatment of addiction disorders along the same lines of any other progressive chronic disease that we doctors treat.

Second addiction treatment services must be integrated into any other medical service provided in clinics, private doctors' offices, and hospitals. I believe it is very important to have MAT readily available in *all* ERs! Many patients end up in the ER when they overdose on opioids and standard practice in ERs is to reverse the overdose and then discharge the patient. It is at this critical moment when the patient is in the ER that Suboxone or methadone should be started along with a direct referral to an addiction medicine specialist and/ or a methadone clinic. Once the patient is started on Suboxone or methadone in the ER, they can be transferred to a private or public medical practice specializing in addiction disorders and then continue to keep patient on MAT (methadone or Suboxone) on a regular maintenance basis with regular follow monthly visits.

I have many patients who overdosed on heroin and/or opioid pills and were treated in the ER with Narcan (this medication reverses opioid overdoses) and, within hours, were back on the street using heroin or opioid pills. There is a new trend in treating opioid overdoses in the ER which involves having recovery coaches (these are folks with past hx drug addictions who are in solid recovery) and are assigned to each overdose patient to make sure they get all necessary follow-up treatments. Oftentimes, the recovery coach will accompany patients to their first doctor visit after their overdose. In the acute stages of recovery, especially after an overdose, it is imperative someone monitor these patients until they are in an established treatment program.

Third, all third-party insurance companies need to eliminate all pre-authorization requirements to be prescribed Suboxone. When a patient presents to the pharmacy with a prescription for Suboxone, it should be approved like any other medication used to treat any other chronic medical condition. I have had patients relapse on heroin because insurance companies delayed filling my Suboxone Rx causing patients to experience withdrawal symptoms, sending them back for more heroin just to calm the withdrawal symptoms. Patients have extreme difficulty tolerating opioid withdrawal symptoms; and thus, they will resort to whatever means necessary to eliminate their withdrawal symptoms. Active withdrawal symptoms render most patients nonfunctional and unable to carry on their normal activities of daily living.

There are many additional barriers to treatment that are beyond the scope of this book, but each barrier is surmountable if we approach addiction use disorders as we do all other chronic progressive disease. *All doctors need* formal training in addiction use disorders and management of chronic pain disorders regardless of their specialty. There are many legitimate patients with chronic pain syndrome who have benefited from opioid pain meds without becoming addicted to these meds. Addiction is different from physiological dependency with the former leading to a continued craving to use opioids where the latter is a normal physiological response to sudden withdrawal of the opioid without a proper taper. When patients with physiological dependency get weaned off their opioids, they have no further cravings to continue using their opioid pain pills.

Public education on any addictive use disorder is another essential avenue that must be maximized to educate our general public. The public must be made aware that addiction disorders are genetically inherited brain disorders influenced by one's psychosocial environment. The general public must also be made aware that there are many effective treatment options especially MATs for a variety of substance use disorders, including opioid use disorder (OUD), Suboxone, methadone, Vivitrol, alcohol use disorder (AUD), and smoking (nicotine replacement therapy).

We are now developing vaccines that can be used to treat cocaine disorders by having the body create specific antibodies that bind to cocaine molecules, making them too large to pass through the blood brain barrier (this is the wall that lets small molecules like cocaine enter the central nervous system and thus getting patients high). Vaccines now will prevent the cocaine molecule from ever crossing the blood brain barrier. If the brain doesn't perceive a positive effect when using a drug, it will stop craving the drug. Soon, there will be vaccines for every specific drug of abuse which will then be given to patients, so they can't get high if they use their specific drug that they are now immunized to.

CHAPTER 7

What Does Recovery Mean to Me and My Patients?

Recovery is the final end product of a successful opioid addiction treatment program. Addiction is the hijacking of the brain's natural mood and feeling regulating system. With chronic use of opioids, the cerebral cortex (the brain area for conscious voluntary control of behavior) becomes subordinate to the primitive sub cortical brain centers (involuntary behavior), causing opiate-dependent patients to "lose control." These patients will experience intense cravings and continue to use opiates despite having negative health and social consequences. Recovery is about restoring the natural, spontaneous, and healthy regulation of mood and feelings; thus, reversing the addiction hijacking process.

Recovery is more than just being free of using opiate(s) of abuse, it also is an attitude and lifestyle change where the patient regains control of his social, psyche, and physical environments. The recovering patient now understands the triggers for his/her past drug use and has developed conscious behaviors for avoiding relapse when exposed to certain triggers. Recovering patients have relearned how to "live life on life's terms" and know how to work through their problems without using mood-altering chemicals.

Once patients have achieved sustained recovery, they develop a new perspective on life in general. They come to appreciate many of the things they ignored when they were in their active drug-using state. Many of their previous negative behaviors disappear and are replaced by healthy positive reinforcing behaviors. In my experience, those patients who have been properly evaluated and treated for comorbid conditions, prescribed appropriate meds for their primary addiction disorder (to eliminate withdrawal symptoms, cravings, and block reinforcing effects of their opiate of abuse), undergone intensive behavioral therapy, and monitored for compliance with random drug screens, achieve the best rates of sustained and meaningful recovery. Finally, another predictor of long-term recovery is the extent a recovering patient reaches out to help other addicted patients.

Of course, any patient in recovery is at risk for relapse regardless of how long they have been in recovery. Many patients relapse multiple times before they finally achieve lasting recovery. Relapse in itself does not mean failure but rather signifies that the treatment plan must be modified to better fit the needs of the particular patient. As with any other chronic disease, many patients with addictions require multiple treatment attempts to finally achieve a well-defined treatment goal. Why then do we label patients with the disease of addiction to be treatment failures when they relapse? Instead, patients who relapse should not be abandoned and written off; but instead, they should be more aggressively pursued and offered more focused treatment.

The benefits of sustained recovery to society are numerous and include significantly reduced health-related cost, decreased criminal activity, reduced incarceration rates, and associated cost and reestablishment of productive taxpaying citizens. However, the most tangible benefits that most recovering patients share with me are the restoration of healthy relationships with family, friends, and coworkers, return of their self-esteem, and regaining control of their lives once again.

Obviously, recovery is an achievable endpoint in many individuals with the disease of addiction. However, we as a society must understand that labeling addicted persons as criminals instead of as patients with a treatable brain disease is an exercise in futility, costing this country billions of dollars. I am convinced that our tax dollars should be directed toward treatment, education, prevention, and research to identify and help addicted persons instead of directing funds for criminalization and incarceration to catch and punish these patients. Once we remove the stigma and criminalization of addiction, redirect funding efforts, and bring addiction treatment into mainstream medicine (as any other chronic disease), we will then be able to contain the current epidemic of addiction use disorders in our society.

ABOUT THE AUTHOR

Dr. Richard A. Campana is a board certified/fellow in addiction medicine who specializes in medically assisted treatment (MAT) for opioid addiction disorders. He has successfully treated thousands of patients using methadone or Suboxone, enabling his patients to live a normal productive life.

Dr. Campana was raised in Williamsburg, Va and started the first urgent care center in Williamsburg in 1984. He transitioned to his current specialty of addiction medicine fifteen years ago. Dr. Campana is a proponent of exercise and wellness as a major part of any patient's recovery as he himself is a long-distance runner.

Dr. Campana is also an avid dog lover and is currently in the early stages of starting a senior dog sanctuary in Virginia. All proceeds from this book will go to the nonprofit organization called *Senior Dog Sanctuary of Virginia*.

CPSIA information can be obtained
at www.ICGtesting.com
Printed in the USA
BVHW030729150820
585881BV00020B/15